Pisces

THIS BOOK BELONGS TO:

_____

THE WONDERFUL WORLD OF ZODIACS

PISCES

Mimi Jones

Dedicated to my aunt, Lori.

All rights reserved.
No part of this book may be reproduced in any form or by any means, electronic or mechanical, and no photocopying or recording, unless you have written permission from the author.

ISBN 978-1-958985-61-8

Text copyright © 2025 by Mimi Jones

www.joeysavestheday.com

A Mimi Book

WELCOME TO:
THE WONDERFUL WORLD OF ZODIACS

PISCES

Mimi Jones

Dates:

Pisces spans from February 19 to March 20.

♓ Ruling Planet: ♓

Neptune and Jupiter rule Pisces.

Symbol:

The Fish represent Pisces.

Pisces

Personality:

Pisceans are known for being compassionate and imaginative.

Strength:

They are very intuitive and empathetic.

Color:

Their lucky colors are sea green, lavender, and pale pink.

Pisces

Lucky Numbers:

3, 7, 12, and 16 are lucky for Pisces.

Compatibility:

Pisces gets along well with Cancer, Scorpio, Taurus, and Capricorn.

CANCER

SCORPIO

TAURUS

CAPRICORN

Career:

They excel in careers that require creativity and empathy.

Positive Trait:

Pisceans are very kind and selfless.

Kind

Negative Trait:

Sometimes, they can be too escapist or overly trusting.

Motto:

Their motto is "I believe."

Favorite Day:

Thursday is their favorite day.

THURSDAY

PISCES

Health:

Pisceans should take care of their feet and immune system.

Famous Pisceans:

Some famous Pisceans include Rihanna, Albert Einstein, and Kurt Cobain.

Challenges:

Pisceans need to learn to set boundaries and stay grounded.

Friendship:

They are deeply caring friends who provide endless support.

Influence:

They inspire others with their creativity and compassion.

Be Creative

Favorite Activities:

Pisceans love activities that involve art, spirituality, and daydreaming.

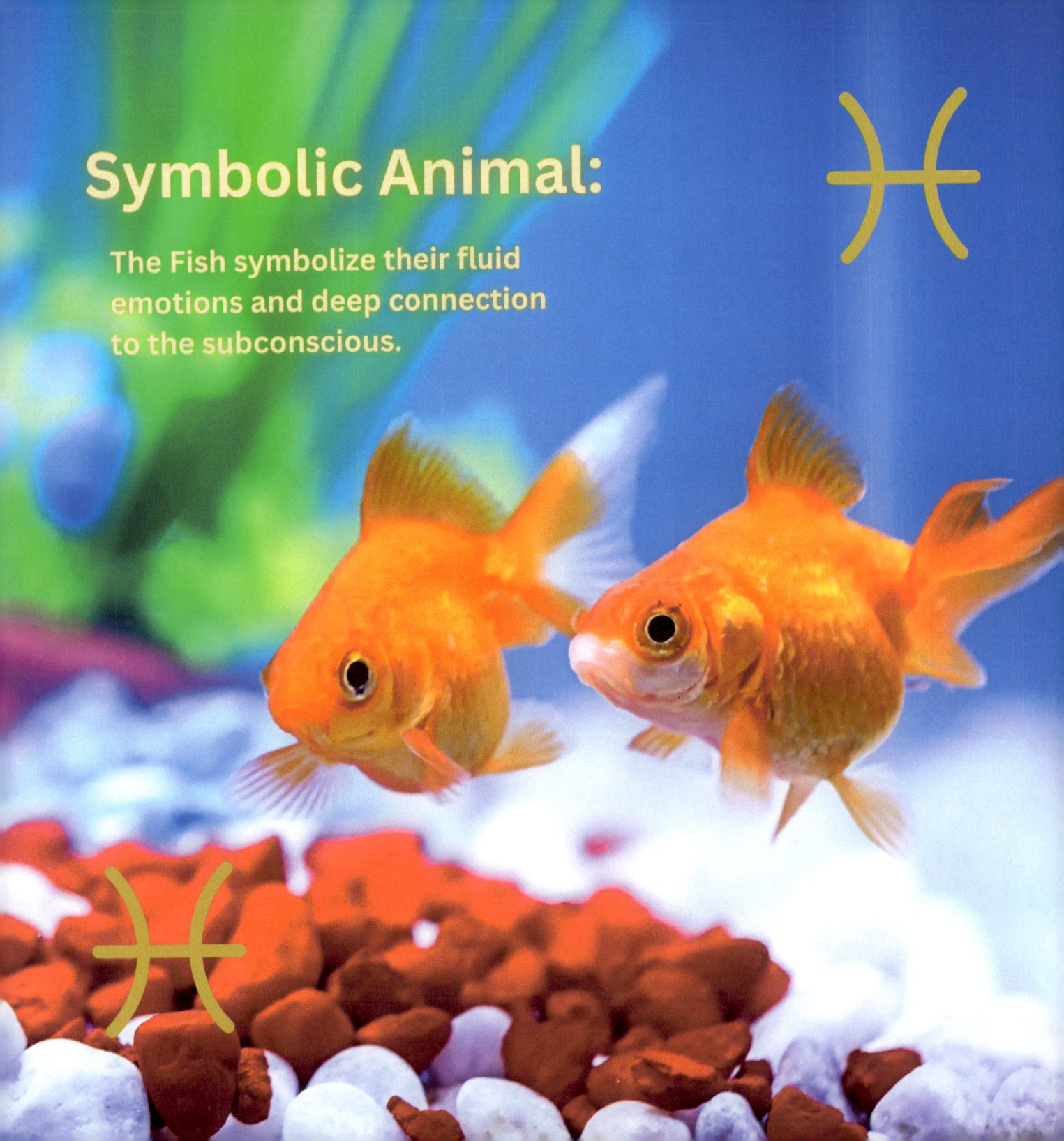

Symbolic Animal:

The Fish symbolize their fluid emotions and deep connection to the subconscious.

Birthstones:

Amethyst and bloodstone.

If this Zodiac gem tickled your celestial fancy, then you're in for a treat! Dive into my other Zodiac delights right here:

www.mimibooks.com

THE END!

www.ingramcontent.com/pod-product-compliance
Lightning Source LLC
Chambersburg PA
CBHW040030050426
42453CB00002B/67